echo

oceans
of
inspiration

Heart Echoes for Living a Life of Joy

SIERRA GOODMAN

oceans
of
inspiration

Heart Echoes for Living a Life of Joy

DIVINE DOLPHIN PUBLICATIONS
©2012 Divine Dolphin

All rights reserved under International and
Pan-American Copyright conventions. Published in the
United States of America by Divine Dolphin Publications.

Book Design by India Redman

ISBN 978-0-615-73014-1
Library of Congress Control Number: 2012954450

OCEANS OF INSPIRATION:
HEART ECHOES FOR LIVING A LIFE OF JOY

FIRST PRINTING

This Book is Dedicated

To my parents who have been so loving and supportive throughout my life. I love you and appreciate you more than you could ever know.

To my brother and internet angel, Lee, thank you for all the magic you do on my behalf from the nonphysical. I KNOW that is YOU!

To my Divine Sacred Soul Sisters, you know who you are, and I am blessed to be traveling this amazing magical journey with you. I Love You. I.K.E.A.

To my dear friend and designer, India Redman, you made this book so easy and did such first class work that I think I'll do another very soon. Thank you.

To my dear Marilyn Umbach, who long ago taught me the Universal Laws, tricks and tools for creating what I want in life and helped formed who I AM now. You are loved and cherished beyond words.

And to the divine dolphins, whales and all the animals who have taught me so much and enrich my life daily. I am blessed to be in your presence. Thank you. Thank you. Thank you.

Introduction

You might wonder who I am to write a "Human Handbook." My qualification is that I am a human being having an authentic human experience, sharing the inner guidance, the echoes of my heart, I receive along the way. I write the things I write as the guidance that is given to me from my own Divine Spirit Connection, my inner guidance, as I am having my human experiences and tune in for answers. I don't share these quotes, messages, Heart Echoes as a guru or master talking AT people. If I am talking AT anyone, it is ME! We All need to be reminded who we are during the course of life's experiences and I am sure I will be referencing this book just as much, if not more, than anyone else. Practice makes permanent. Or at least much more often. We ARE deliciously human after all. That's the fun of it!

Life isn't about some kind of self-inflected ideal of perfection or 'stuff' not happening, it's about how you deal with the stuff that happens. It's in how you choose to feel about it. It's about being your authentic self. It's in embracing and loving your human self and finding the perfect blend of body, mind and spirit that is your balance point of Joy. It's in mining the golden nuggets from experiences and leaving the rest behind. It's in being observant of what you choose to focus on and believe and talk about over and over. It's trusting in the divine timing and orchestration of the Universe. It's about THE SHIFT and becoming a better and faster shifter. It's about letting go — and a word I used to hate — surrender. Not giving up, mind you, but Surrendering to the Divine. And it's about not taking it all so seriously. In fact, not taking much seriously at all. A life of JOY is our birthright. Well, I just about summed up the whole book in one paragraph!

People call me lucky because of my warm-tropical-rainforest-ocean front-swim with dolphins and whales-fun and free lifestyle, but it's not luck that got me here. It has been conscious co-creating with The Divine, asking for and allowing for the Highest Good for All Concerned, letting go of the outcome... and letting the Universe deliver something even better than I could have imagined. And do I still want more? Heck yes! It is the beautiful human condition to want MORE. So bring on Tarzan already!

This book is yours to use as your heart and divine guidance leads. You might want to completely read through once and then use it for daily inspiration and messages — randomly turning to a page that will surely say just what you need to hear. The Universe is magical like that, giving us just what we need, when we need it.

It is my Deepest Divine Desire that this collection of my *Heart Echoes* brings you the inspiration and messages you need *when* you need them — whether that is a soft, gentle reminder or a swift kick in the butt, or what I like to call a "clue by four." May you always feel the immense joy and unconditional love from which this book is birthed. It is my heartfelt desire that you are happy, successful and living the life of your dreams. You are worthy and loved.

As you read these *Heart Echoes* through different life experiences, they will have new meanings for you and speak to you on different levels as you grow and expand and come to deeper and broader understandings.

When I talk about God/the Universe/Spirit/The Divine in this book, I use them interchangeably in an attempt to describe, in words, the Super Intelligence that is the constant stream of Unconditional Love, Wellbeing and Wisdom that we ALL ARE.

I have infused this book with LOTS of Love and Light and have visualized and sent LOVE to every single person who will hold it in their hands, so even carrying it with you will provide loving support to you in your daily life.

It's SHOWTIME, BABY!

Many blessings and Oceans of Love,

Sierra

oceans *of* inspiration

Heart Echoes for Living a Life of Joy

SIERRA GOODMAN

I came here

for the human game,

and I play it with Joy!

When you judge

others, you are judging
an aspect of YOU.
Instead focus on
BEING the Divine Spark
of Divine Expression
that YOU are.
Allow the spice of life.
Allow ALL the beautiful
and unique expressions
of the Divine.
FEEL the ONEness with others.
It is WHO YOU ARE.

We are ALL channelers…

Whenever we are allowing Pure Source/God Energy to FLOW THROUGH us, when we are "on our game" or "in the zone," we are channeling Source. When words, music, poetry, art, uncontrollable laughter flow through us, we are channeling Source. When we are making love, when we are present in the moment, when we are in appreciation, when we are feeling and sharing unconditional love, we are channeling Spirit. So basically, just by being, everyone is channeling/flowing Spirit in their own unique way…

When you are

observing something that doesn't please you, instead of complaining about what everyone else is doing wrong, either remove yourself from the situation or BE the change you want to see… Otherwise you are always giving your power over to others because you are needing them to change for things to be right in your world. Take your power back and remember that what you see around you is a reflection of what you are focused on. If you need things to change, that change comes from within first.

YOU are the power.

We are All

Swimming

in an Infinite

Ocean of

Possibilities!

Allow your beliefs

and who you are to evolve as you
live out the authentic human
experience. Try not to be too rigid in
your thinking and stay stuck in a box
of how things are... Once you define
it, you have boxed it in. Allow for
new ideas and perspectives to evolve
and expand your horizons, dreams
and ways of being... Grow and Glow!

You are not

responsible for nor can you control
the way that others react to your
words and actions. You are only
responsible for and can control the
vibration from which you deliver
them. Don't get pulled in or allow
others to run their patterns,
insecurities, dramas, expectations
and their old and repetitive stories
on you. Stay in the vibration of
LOVE and PLAY and if necessary,
walk away! Or Swim Away!!

We came here

for the human experience but yet people fight and resist their ego. The ego is what keeps us grounded in our humanness. The ego is the difference between the human mind and the Divine mind and it is not about one or the other. It's about a perfect blending of the two for the authentic human experience of a spiritual being in a human body. Our ego is what defines our unique personality and desires. The ego is not to be pushed away and erased but embraced.

To hold on

to hurt and blame

is to give your power

over to others.

THEY are not suffering,

YOU are.

Let it go and

take your power back!

If you are always

seeking a state of constant Bliss or
Happiness, you will always be
seeking. And when you realize that
it's ALL blissfully part of the human
experience, even what we have
labeled as bad and unfair, and you
stay present in your heart, you will
never have to seek again.

It's an inside job.

Isn't it time

to step out of your comfort zone and
expand into more? Isn't it time you
lived your dream instead of just
dreaming it? Isn't it time you
stopped caring about what others
think more than what YOU think?
Isn't it time to be true to YOU? Like,
really... WHAT ARE YOU
WAITING FOR?

Everything happens

in Divine Timing and Orchestration...

trust THAT

and you let in

all the Magic and Ease

of the Universe!

Linear Time

exists only as an illusion for our

personal growth and expansion...

and for organization of events.

In the REAL reality, Past, Present

and Future all exist

RIGHT NOW.

So by being Happy NOW you create

your fate today, tomorrow and

yesterday. This NOW moment is all

there is.

Now. NOW. NOW!!!

So forget the How. Be in the Now.

And make it WOW!!

When you are

the observer,

present

and connected to

the moment,

all there is

is Love.

You cannot not be

spiritual, for you are a spiritual being... more non physical than physical. You cannot not channel, for you are always channeling and expressing God/Source/Spirit through you. You cannot get it wrong as every choice is a valuable experience and expands you. You cannot not love, for it is who you are and where you came from. You are all this and so much more…

LET It In, LET It In,

LET IT IN!!

You are a Divine

Spiritual Being

worthy of all

that you desire

and more.

Any questions?

Limiting Beliefs

are like weeds

in the garden

of your mind.

Pick them out

so that new,

unlimited beliefs

can grow!

BE the Light

It feels so Right

Give up the Fight

Time to take Flight

And Shine it BRIGHT!

The more you blame

and judge others,
the easier it is to look away from
those very qualities in yourself.
Instead, use what bothers you about
others as an opportunity to look
inside and see if there is something
you are not loving about yourself.

I love you.

Everything is

always happening for your

highest good...

you can relax and trust that...

or you can fight it all the way and

keep trying and thinking your

way through.

But life is MUCH easier when you

let go and go with the flow and

allow Divine timing and

orchestration to do it's thang!

It's when you allow

Source to flow

THROUGH you,

that magic happens.

Be a vessel for Love, Joy and

Wellbeing to flow through and out

into the world.

Every moment

spent thinking negative thoughts
about something not wanted or
talking about something or
someone not desired and telling
the same story over and over,
is precious time that could be
spent creating, visualizing,
intending and taking action on
what you DO desire!

It's ALL spiritual!

Anything and everything is a spiritual experience because after all, we are spiritual beings. You cannot NOT be spiritual! We can let go of seeking answers, comfort and Love outside of ourselves otherwise we will always be seeking that "spiritual experience." Rituals, ceremonies, seminars… all fun and certainly it is always powerful when people come together in conscious focus. But there is no right way or one way. Just do what you love, live life to the fullest, follow your heart and intuition and have lots and lots and lots of FUN. That's about as Divine of a "spiritual" experience as there is.

Leggo your ego,

for it serves you in wanting
and creating more...
Embrace your monkey mind,
for it serves you to expand
and learn more...
Let go of the resistance
and pushing against...
You are perfect and whole with all
the right parts.
There is nothing to fix or keep in
check. Just stay in your Love/Heart
Center and all the right parts work at
the right time in the right balance.
It's who you Divinely are.

Pods, flocks, packs, herds...

the animals know we are not meant
to do this alone. We are meant to be
in community, in communication
and communing with our tribes. It is
in the authentic human sharing and
interactions that we expand and
grow. We build on each other's
experiences and talents and zones of
genius. It is okay and necessary to
need others... without being needy.
It's part of the human experience.
Bring your true, authentic, brightest
self to the mix and watch how your
clan expands and how you light
each other's fires!!

IN-LIGHT-IN-ment

happens when you stop

seeking the Divine

outside yourself

and embrace

the Divine Shine within.

Always let

your vibration speak for itself. You
don't have to defend yourself or tell
your side of the story to those who
are quick to judge or not interested
in your perspective. Trust the vibe to
work it all out. Just keep shining on,
loving on and blessing on and leave
the drama to reality TV...

Gently guide

yourself towards your dreams in all your waking hours. Be your own observer. Lovingly ask yourself: Will the action I am about to take bring me in the direction that I want to go? Are my dreams and desires and visions for the highest good for all concerned? Are the thoughts I am thinking what I want to create? Are the words I am speaking in line with who I really am? If not, gently and with love, make the shift in focus and action and get back on the Dream Train, Baby!

I follow

my guidance,

I do what feels good to me

and therefore I am always

led to the best possible outcome!

If you believe

you can't be happy

until you are rich or thin

or in a relationship, those things will

not bring you happiness even if you

get them. You have to have a solid

base of self worth and happiness

FIRST and then those things can

come faster and enhance your

already joyful life.

Jealousy

of others shows a feeling of lack, that

there is not enough to go around or

that you are less than.

There is no lack.

There is no less than.

There is abundance and success and

health and relationships and love

enough for everyone.

You will always

see evidence of what you believe. If
you believe nothing ever works out
for you, you will see plenty of
evidence of that. If you change your
old story and instead believe that you
were born under a lucky star, you
will see evidence of that. Change your
beliefs and the evidence that appears
in your life will change too.

If you know

that what you focus on

you are creating more of,

why stay stuck in the muck? Yuck!!

Let it go and GROW!!

Oh us humans.

Why do we ever stay in relationships; love, work or otherwise, that do not nourish our souls? Maybe we think we don't deserve better. Maybe we think we can help or save these people. Maybe we just get comfortable with the uncomfortable. Maybe we are forever waiting for "the right time." Maybe we think tomorrow will be different or if we just hold our high vibration it will be okay. But all of this at what expense to our own joy and happiness and self-respect and tranquility and peace? Every single time I have finally retreated from a relationship that was no longer nourishing my soul, I say every time, "What took me so long?" The feelings of release and freedom and LIGHTness sooth my soul immediately. And here's the great part. EVERYONE goes off to their HIGHEST GOOD!!! What is good for you is good for others, even if they don't see it at the time. ALL is in Divine Orchestration; we can't take away someone else's Good… EVER!… And when we take control of our joy and happiness and peace and tranquility by stepping away from that which does not feel good, it gets REALLY REALLY GOOD!!! Sooooo GOOD!!

We don't have to

figure out the how or when... that is
the work of the Universe. Our work
is to dream the dream, getting into
the feeling place of it being DONE,
and then let it go like we KNOW it
is already done... because it is,
even better than we could
have imagined!

I fully let in

all that is Divine

and in time

and I fully release

all that is no longer mine.

Our power

of choice

is our creative power.

In every moment,

in every situation,

in every relationship and job,

we have a choice

about how we feel

and therefore

what we create

in our experience.

Even when it seems

that things didn't work out,

it worked out...

Trust in the Divine

orchestration and timing

of the Universe

and the Higher Good

and things will

ALWAYS

work out for you.

Life does not

just happen to you.

You happen to life.

Embrace your creative power and

focus given to you

as your Divine birthright

by Pure Love Source.

Wishy Washy

focus, thoughts and desires

get wishy washy results.

Get clear,

get focused

and watch how

your path becomes clear

and focused too!

You don't have to

"create" anything.

For if you have thought it,

if you have dreamed it,

it already exists,

it has already been created.

Allow it in.

Simply step into it.

Open the door and

walk right in!

Honor ALL

your emotions... do not resist or fight
them. Allow yourself to be afraid, to
be angry, to FEEL what you feel.
Resisting does not get rid of them, it
makes them get bigger. As soon as
we allow ourselves to FEEL them is
when shifting from them is possible.
It's really, really okay to be human &
have human emotions.
It's all perfectly perfect for your
journey and growth.
DO NOT SUPPRESS... EXPRESS!!

We came

to EXPERIENCE the Authentic Human Experience. To laugh, cry, dance, love, scream, be silent & FEEL. Revel in it ALL. Bask in the tears and in the laughter. Don't cheat yourself by trying to "ascend" and "enlighten" and "seek" your life away. This isn't about ascending; it is about bringing Heaven to Earth. This isn't about seeking; it is about embracing who you already ARE. A truly enlightened being is one who is balanced & blended in their non-physical AND physical selves, living life authentically as a grounded human BEing.
JUST BE.
Enjoy and bask in your NOW, your physical human NOW.

Bless the human

angels who come into your life,
as mutually agreed, to cause you to
remember more of who you really
are. Bless the ones who you allowed
to make you feel angry and hurt for
they are the ones who give us the
biggest opportunity for growth and
expansion. The key is to not get stuck
in the hurt or the anger, but to look
within to what was triggered and
heal thyself with LOVE.
Bless them all… for they give us
strength, courage, clarity and the
never-ending opportunity to
BE LOVE.

Listen, Divine Beings

and you will hear,
Your own Inner Guidance
loud and clear.

You are the one who
knows what's best for you.
So follow your heart,
to your authentic self be true.

There is nothing to obtain,
no one you have to be.
You have it all inside you,
so set yourself free.

In the present moment
is where you find your true self.
Past stories and present worries
remain on the shelf.

To follow your dreams
is what you came here for.
So get passionate, BE Possibility
and wait no more.

[more]

Instead of complaining and
waiting for change,
Refocus your NOW
and watch your life rearrange.

Let go of the baggage
and the attachments too.
Cause' once resistance is gone,
it's a dream life for you.

Let go of the hurt,
let go of the blame.
And start living your life
in charge of the game.

Be FOR, not against,
speak from love and respect.
This is how you create
the Love Consciousness Effect.

When things don't
go how you think they should,
Remember there is the Law
of The Highest Good.

[more]

The higher perspective,
the Divine Broader View,
is how it can all
make sense to you.

Allow unique perspectives
and inspired Source to flow.
Every Being has their unique journey
to expand and to grow.

Trust in Divine timing,
let the Universe orchestrate.
And it all turns out better
than your imagination could create.

Know you are worthy,
embrace your Divine.
Expect the best to happen,
for it happens all the time!

Live from the heart,
be the LOVE that you ARE.
And your true and authentic self
will shine like a star.

There is a difference

between having personal
preferences and judgment. There is
a difference between "I see it this
way" or "That's not for me" and
"You are wrong." It's okay to prefer
what you prefer; we came here
with unique perspectives and
preferences... just allow others to
have theirs!

Taking inspired

action towards your dreams and
desire is your testimonial to the
Universe that you believe in
yourself and your dreams and trust
enough to MOVE for them and that
allows the Universe to move
mountains for you!!

We don't have to

lure, control or try hard to make
things happen. When we are focused
on the essence of our vision, we can
let go of things having to be a certain
way. Trust and let the Universe do
its Divine Timing and
Orchestration thing.

BECOME

that which you seek,

and that which you seek

will BECOME you!

Trust yourself.

Trust those nudges,

trust that little voice,

trust your gut,

trust your intuition

and most of all,

trust your HEART!

Maybe you think

you don't make a difference...
but there has never been a time
like now where EVERY
VIBRATION COUNTS!
YOU contribute to the collective
vibration of the YOUniverse... You
don't have to do something "big"
to make a difference... shining
your light and living from your
heart IS BIG!

May you today

know your Brilliance

May you know your Divinity

May you shine your Light

May you feel the Love

May you experience Great Joy

May you see the Magic in Everything

May you embrace Grace

Today.

May you allow

in the beauty and grace that

surrounds you, no matter where you

are and what you are doing...

Smile, bask, appreciate,

feel the LOVE that IS

and that you ARE...

and let Spirit

shine through YOU!

There is no

such thing as failure,

only new information.

Follow your inspired dreams

no matter what!

Live a life

of integrity,

not only to others,

but most of all

to yourself and your soul.

Be your authentic self!

People get caught

up in things having to be a certain

way to feel a certain way.

Feel how you want to feel and let

the Universe bring to you the things

that match it that might

or might not be how

you thought it would be.

I shall no longer

hide from my light. I shall no longer argue for my limitations. I fully accept, honor and carry out my Divine plan and service to humanity without resistance (except for when it comes up and then I shall joyfully do the work to name it, claim it & release it.) I easily and gracefully step into my agreed upon Divine Role and I fully embrace Who I Really Am.

I shine my light with pure love and compassion & work with my tribe to create true community.

I AM HERE. NOW.

Humans

put a lot of conditions on what love
should look like and feel like. But the
truth is, it is ALL love... and
sometimes the disagreements and
anger are the most passionate
I Love You's of All.

Passionate

Intention

is the

Mother of Invention.

We live

in an amazing,

magical Universe.

Go outside and connect

with nature; watch the clouds create

shapes, listen to the birds sing their

songs, watch a sunset, walk

barefoot....

and you will find your connection to

All That Is!

It starts

with faith and trust...

then comes believing...

and then comes knowing...

and then comes implementing and

integrating what you know and

BEING IT...

and that's where the real

magic happens!

If you are standing

strong in your high vibration and
heart space, no outside influences
and energies can affect you and come
into your "space." Don't look outside
yourself if you are not feeling good.
Don't blame others or the "energies"
around you. It is only from within,
and the vibration that we put out that
determines how we feel.

In other words,

YA CAN'T TOUCH THIS!

We never have to

jump through vibrational hoops for
anyone or acquiesce to their ideas of
how a relationship should be based
upon the boxes of rules they have
built around them. We never have to
be drawn into others dramas,
pettiness, insecurities, resistance or
judgments. We never ever ever have
to play small for others.
Play BIG, or go home!

Others real

or perceived judgments can only
affect you if you are already judging
yourself. It is only if you are afraid
there is some truth in it that it can
break you or shake you. Usually the
judgments we think are happening
are created in our minds because of
our insecurities and others mirroring
that. Let go of your inner critic and
all the other critics, real or imagined,
will disappear from your reality.

Today

instead of talking about what you
don't like, what others are doing
wrong (from your perspective) and
basically focusing on what you don't
want... talk about and focus on what
you do like and want. It will change
your whole day...
AND the added bonus?
You will get MORE of
what you like and want
simply by focusing on it!

Just because

people are taking action towards

what they feel is right doesn't mean

they haven't looked within.

Perhaps when they looked within

their heart told them,

"Go and be a part

of the change."

I am a big believer

in the power of writing things down
and sending our desires out into the
Universe. Yes, write down your
dreams and goals, but then STEP
OUT OF THE WAY and let go of the
outcome as it can be and usually is
MUCH BIGGER AND BETTER
THAN YOU EVER
COULD HAVE DREAMED.
Don't limit yourself to your lists,
let DIVINE ORCHESTRATION
take over.

Don't add

"but I don't have the money"
to your visions, dreams and desires.
Stay true to your dreams and
passion and watch the money,
resources, people and places appear
like magic in ways you couldn't have
imagined. Forget the how.
Be in the NOW!

It is natural

for you to have desire and it is
natural for you to anticipate happy
outcomes and it is natural for you to
Love, and it is natural for you to sing
and dance and it is natural for you to
play. It is natural for you to skip, it is
natural for you to be joyful, it is
natural for you to know wellbeing, it
is natural for you to expand, it is
natural to feel. It is natural for you to
question, it is natural for you to find
interest, it is natural for you to want
more and it is natural for you to feel
good… and anything else is resisting
the natural state of who you are.

Is there a story

You've been telling about your life
(job, relationships, health) for too
long now that holds you back from
where you want to be? Well, STOP
IT! Telling the same story over and
over holds you right where you
don't want to be... in that story! But
speaking of the positive aspects of
your life and joyously speaking
about your dreams and telling a
NEW STORY moves you towards
where you want to go. Telling a new
story with passion raises your
vibration so much that your new
story can became your new reality.
Image-in the possibilities!

Most of us

already have all the tools and
techniques we need to release
resistance to our divinity and feelings
of unworthiness, however our
patterns of self-sabotage and upper
limits of self-worth and success keeps
us from doing them. Most of us do
not finish courses, exercises that
would help us if we did. But we keep
searching anyway so that we have an
excuse to not integrate what we
already know. It's time to stop
playing Hide n' Go Seek. It's time to
integrate and BE who we already are
and what we already know.

You cannot miss

an opportunity that is yours by
Divine right. You cannot lose what is
for your highest good. There are
infinite doors and possibilities along
your journey… so let go of things
having to be a certain way or the
need for specific outcomes. When
you stop focusing on what didn't
happen and what you don't have and
instead trust in the infinite love and
benevolence of Spirit and the
Universe and focus on what you
WANT, you will live a life full of
abundance and prosperity on all
levels… and the outcomes will be
better than you could have ever
imagined.

It's time

to BE FREE! It's time to stop seeking
and trying. You don't have to follow
some ritual or certain sequence or
secret formula to connect to YOU.
There is no special ceremony and you
don't have to go to India or Tibet or
meditate for hours to
BE AUTHENTICALLY YOU.
Spirituality is not a religion with
rules and rituals to follow.
SPIRIT-U-ality is who you ARE.
Right NOW! Even before you take
that next course, class or cruise... You
have it NOW! No more excuses. No
more giving away your power to
other people or things. YOU ARE IT!
Now go LIGHT UP THE WORLD!

Things might not

turn out how you thought they

should; people may not be there like

you thought they would...

but know, oh do know, that

ALL is in Divine order

and for the highest GOOD!

We already have

all the tools and techniques and

teachings we need to fully BE who

we really are. It's time to stop

playing Hide n' Go Seek

with our spirituality.

It's time to integrate and BE what we

already know and who we already

are. Come out, come out,

wherever you are!

It doesn't take

a rocket science to figure out where
you are vibrating on any given
subject. Just look at your bank
account, your relationships, your
career...what you are getting is what
you are vibrating. And if you are not
getting what you want, you have
beliefs and patterns that are keeping
you where you are. Bust the beliefs,
shift the patterns and you are free!

You ARE love

in every moment, it's where you

came from and who you are.

Whether you are tuned in to it or

not is your choice...

Tune in to love!

Breathe Deeply

& Connect ~ Act from Inspiration ~
Follow Your Heart ~ Trust Your
Intuition ~ Know Your Divinity ~
Have FUN ~ Let Go & Surrender to
Divine Order & Orchestration ~
Dream BIG, then BIGGER ~
Laugh A LOT ~
Allow In Your Good ~
Know Your Worthiness ~
Stay Present to the Moment ~
BE LOVE ~

Only share

your dreams and visions with

other unlimited thinkers who

inspire and support you.

Don't say a word to

Debbie Doubters and

Donald Dream Dashers!

Most of us

Didn't come here to meditate our
lives away in a cave and get all
spiritual and enlightened in that
way... we came here to experience
the physical human experience...
ALL of it! The laughter, the tears, the
joy, the anger... ALL of it! Living a
Life of Joy is not about challenges
not arising... it's about loving it ALL
and constantly shifting to the higher,
broader perspective because you
know that everything is in Divine
order and orchestration... that's how
you stay joyful and enlightened!

It has been

demonstrated to me
once again how gracefully
misunderstandings,
misinterpretations and misguided
projections, expectations and
resentments can be very easily
cleaned up and cleared up with
open, honest, authentic
communication from both sides. Just
say what you need to say… and say
it from your heart with LOVE.

Once you really

start embracing YOUR unique

human experience, you will stop

caring or comparing yourself to what

others are doing.

You just are not doing this

human thing wrong.

You are doing it YOUR way...

and that's alright with me!

Never wish

ill will upon others, no matter what you
think they have done, as it will surely
come back to you though the web of
inter-connection. Because we are all
ONE, all intimately and eternally
intertwined and connected, we must
wish the highest and best for everyone,
even our enemies and those who do not
wish it for you, and especially them.

The highest and best for others is
always the highest and best for you too.
Spread only good will and good wishes
through our inter-connected web of life.
Make LOVE be your contribution to
the WHOLE.

Of course

we all have the Divine Spark within
without using any tools or toys or
mantras and meditations... but OH! It's
so fun to play and interact and expand
with other Divine Sparks, whether that
be human, rock, animal, plant,
material, other dimension, out of this
world Sparks. It's about seeing the
Divine Spark in everything and
anything... and PLAY accordingly.
Nature has POWER... PLAY with it!
Listen! Feel!! Do nothing or do
whatever you do with passion and love
and inspiration and the highest
intentions...for ALL concerned. That's
how Divine Sparks
who BE who they truly are set the
world on fire...

You already are

amazing. You already are Divine.
You already are Love. You already
are abundant, healthy, wise,
confident, joyful. You already ARE
all that, and so much more. You
don't have to do anything to be all
these things except embrace that it is
already yours by Divine birthright.

You are the captain

of your own ship. Set your Guidance

Positioning System to LOVE, Joy,

Light, Breezy, Free and Easy and

don't change your course for anyone

or anything! Full steam ahead!!

You are whole

and complete RIGHT NOW. You are already DIVINE LOVE ONENESS. You are already connected, for you cannot be dis-connected, you can only forget that you ARE and WHO you ARE. And you can remember RIGHT NOW. You don't need a teacher, guru or master, you don't need someone to tell you what to do and how to do it. EMBRACE and OWN your DIVINITY and BIRTHRIGHT right NOW. OWN it NOW!! SING it OUT, SHINE it OUT, LAUGH out LOUD, JUMP for JOY, BE your AUTHENTIC TRUE YOU. That is your gift to the world.

Embrace the Divine

Spiritual Being that you are. Allow in
the constant stream of Love always
flowing to you. Celebrate the
magical, mysterious way the
Universe delivers in ways you
couldn't have imagined. Embrace Joy.
Embrace Love. Embrace All that Is.
Embrace YOU!

Trust your Vibes.

Trust when things feel right... and
trust when they don't. Trust when
people move in and out of your life;
some for a season, some for a
lifetime. Trust your body, trust your
intuition and trust in the Divine
timing and orchestration of it all.
Trust your heart and most of all,
trust that you are
loved beyond measure.

What are you giving

more importance to than your own
joy and happiness? Is there a little
blame, anger, hurt, injustice that you
are putting more importance on than
your true state of Joy? Is there a his-
story, her-story, he said, she said,
they did that you keep telling which
keeps you from experiencing your
birthright of wellbeing? Is there
somewhere where you are looking at
what went wrong instead of what
went right, cutting off the LOVE
from your life? Well, Stop It!! It's
time to come back to your Balance
Point of Joy,
Well Being and Love!!

You have all the power

within you to create the life
you desire. What are you thinking
about? What are you visualizing?
What are you feeling? Put ALL your
focus on what you want, and watch
the Universe bend over backwards,
in ways you cannot imagine to give
you all that you desire and more!

It's not just about

being all that you can be...

it's about embracing all that

you already ARE!

Let Go,

Step into the Flow,

and watch your life

Gooooooo!

Many speak of

the "veil" lifting. For me, it is not a matter of some misty veil lifting to reveal what is behind the curtain... there is only being a matching vibration to what is and always has been there. As humans vibrate at higher and higher rates as we are now, what used to be invisible, seemingly behind some veil, becomes visible. More and more people are seeing lights, energies, angels, and so much more previously thought to be "out there" on another plane or in another dimension. They were never out there. They have always been here and now we are coming to the vibrational point that we can see them more easily. More people are accepting and allowing of it too. The supernatural is becoming Super Natural and there is a lot more to come. Bring it on!! Especially the shiny, pretty, sparkly lights and stuff...

There will always be

those who focus on what you're not doing or what they think you should be doing or are doing wrong. It's an easy way to avert their attention from themselves and the mirror you are reflecting to them. Pay no mind to the peanut gallery. Trust YOUR guidance and intuition. Follow YOUR heart. Trust YOUR journey. You don't want to live the life that others want you to life.
Live YOUR life. And do it with confidence and grace…

Everything

I have ever done right or
seemingly wrong at the time
(you can't get it wrong anyway)
has led me up to this powerful
moment of who I am today. I am
eternally appreciative of it all and
WHO I AM because of it!

You can collect

evidence of what is wrong or you
can collect evidence of what is
right. Whichever you choose to
do, you will certainly find more
and more of it to collect.

Why would we ever

want or wish anything less than
LOVE and the very best for
everyone, including those who
oppose us? Because we are ONE,
then LOVE is the only possible
desire for all to experience.
What affects others, affects us.
Wish LOVE upon all,
even those who may not be
wishing Love upon you.
Yes, it starts with YOU!

When your core

belief is that All Is Well, that
everything is happening exactly
as it should, that there is a
higher reason for everything
even when we can't see it, that
everyone is exactly where they
should be on their journey
including YOU, then life
becomes a breeze!

It's great to have

lots of aha's and realizations and
knowings… and then it's
important to take the next steps
which are integration and doing
and BEING whom your expansion
has caused you to become.

Life is like a movie.

God is the Executive Producer and you are the Writer, Director and Actor. You get to choose whether you live action and adventure, horror, romantic comedy or lots of drama and if you are the star or a bit actor in your own life. You get to choose who your co-actors are and if it is an A movie or a B movie. Since you are the writer and director, at any time you can change the scene, the actors, the entire story whenever you want. Take creative control of your life movie. It's time for lights, camera, ACTION!

Yes, it's
SHOW TIME!
And that's a wrap!

INTEGRATION!

It's time. You've done the courses, seminars, workshops, cruises and now is the time to integrate it all into your daily life.

You have all the answers within. You know just what to do. You have the tool box now use the tools.

Observe, Be, Live, Laugh, Love. Break the old patterns and make today the day that is different than business as usual. Yes, today. Fear dissolves into Love. You KNOW who you really are. No more hiding. Shine your light fully and have fun doing it!

Sometimes

unconditional love means loving
from a distance. Sometimes
unconditional love means standing
firm in your high vibration and
shining the light... no matter how
much they kick and scream and
tell you that you don't love them.
Don't mistake joining in other's
low vibration as love. The best
unconditional love you can give is
your high vibe and light so that
others can find their way there too.

Complete Faith

and Trust are the fastest
and easiest way to alignment
with your dreams.
You don't have to "try" to align,
you LET GO to align.
Ask for the highest good for all
concerned and then relax,
KNOWING it is done...
then watch the miracles happen.

If you were living

the life of your dreams, who would
you be? What would you do?
Take a moment to feel how you
would feel if you were living the life
of your dreams.

Doesn't that feel amazing?

But then maybe that little, or not so
little, voice comes in. The one that
says that your dream is out of reach
for you, only achievable by the
charmed and lucky ones; those who
were born with it. You could never
do that. Where would the money
come from?

That is the voice of your limiting
beliefs. It lies there under the
surface, that background (or not)
voice that is sabotaging your

[more]

visualizations, your affirmations, your vision boards, your good intentions and your dreams. It could be that you understand the Universal Laws or different teachings on an intellectual level and you really believe it, but you are not intentionally applying it in your daily life to your benefit.

Well ... it's time to APPLY. It's time to FLY! Allow yourself to observe and gently shift old patterns and beliefs that keep you from GOING FOR IT and living the life of your dreams. Be gentle and patient with yourself. Love yourself a lot. Have FUN with this. Decide to be Happy RIGHT NOW!
Choose it. Own it. Be it.

When we speak

our authentic truth, those on the
receiving end might not always see
us as kind and compassionate. Speak
it anyway. By not speaking up, we
are not being kind and
compassionate to ourselves.
Say it with LOVE and let go of the
outcome. We cannot be all things to
all people, but we CAN be our true
authentic selves no matter what
other people think. It's YOUR life
and YOUR truth!

It's okay

to have preferences and likes and dislikes. You did not come here to vibe with everything and agree with everyone, you came to create your own unique perspective and experience. You don't have to face, fight and figure out everything that doesn't attract or inspire you. HONOR the preferences and beliefs of others and FOCUS on yours.

From fear

comes focus ~
From chaos comes clarity and
calm ~ From experience comes
insight and compassion. Let life's
experiences become stepping
stones and springboards into
becoming so much MORE. Sift
through them for every lesson and
possibility for growth. Let the
lessons flow into more LOVE.
That's what life's experiences are
all about... how much LOVE
can we milk from this?

When we clearly

speak our truth from the heart,
others still have their own filters
and perceptions through which
they hear it. People hear only what
they can and want to hear. So speak
your heart truth and let go of how it
is received. Speak your heart truth
for you and then trust in the
outcome even when it's not what
you thought it might be. When
spoken from the heart, your truth
will always create the highest
possible outcome for you.

Life doesn't

just happen, you make it

happen... and whether shit

happens or miracles happen,

happens to be up to you... and

how you happen to feel about it.

We are all connected

and intertwined by a Divine Web of
Energy, Light and Magical
stardust... Send your Love to each
and every thread, for they are
connected to YOU.

Affirmations,

and faith, etc. work when you don't have a stronger belief that negates them. For instance if you are repeating an affirmation of "I am healthy, wealthy and wise" and the words are coming out of your mouth but your mind is thinking, "No I'm not, that's for other people, things like that never happen to me, I don't deserve it, I'm too fat, lazy, stupid, ugly, etc."... all the negative things we can think and say about ourselves, well then THAT is your dominant vibration, what you are putting out to the Universe, and your affirmation gets canceled out. You might not even realize it because the beliefs of unworthiness have been an underlying current for years (or not so underlying). It might be time to learn to REALLY love yourself and feel your worthiness as the Divine extension of God/Spirit that you are! Then step back and allow the Universe to deliver everything you want and more!

You can say

you want this, and take action
towards that, but vibrating on the
same frequency is where it's all at.
This is a vibrational Universe, and
we can all run but we can't hide
from The Vibe! It's more than what
you say or do that shines through...
it's what vibration you are
ascribing to.

Vibe High!
Love Rulz!
Peace Out!

What is the face

you put out to the world?
What does the bumper sticker you
wear on your forehead say?
Does it say, "Shit Happens" or
"Miracles Happen"? Does it say,
"Baby on Board" or Baby, I'm
bored!"? "Love Stinks" or "Love is
the Answer"? What do you
"Brake" for? The face (and bumper
sticker) you put out in the world is
what is reflected back to you.
So put out YOUR authentic self to
the world and see how many
people Brake for You!

The Universe loves

ACTION!
When you start taking action
towards your dreams, even small
steps, you set into motion the
frequency vibration jumping
molecules that will bring you people,
places and things to get you there
easier and faster. When you take
action towards your dreams and
desires, the Universe knows you
believe in yourself and reciprocates
accordingly.
In other words, DO IT!

Everything you want

or need to know can be found in

your NOW moment.

Your present observation of the

present brings lots of presents!

Holding on

to and living from the past is like
driving along and only looking in
the rear view mirror. Release and
let it go, focus forward and you'll
run into a lot less speed bumps.

Shifting gears into NOW!

We don't have to

go seeking the Light from any

outside sources.

WE ARE THE LIGHT.

Stand right where you are and

turn up the dimmer switch on

your own inner light!

Shift happens...

how you feel about it

is entirely up to you!

The Universe

always speaks to us in OUR
language. Signs and messages
will always come in ways that we
will understand but may mean
nothing for someone else. I am
appreciative that the Universe
speaks to me through nature in
the most creative and amazing
ways. We are all always Divinely
guided. Are you listening?

Is there something

that you are putting off until
tomorrow until a hundred
tomorrows go by? Is there a candle or
a dish or an outfit that you are saving
for a special occasion? Is there
something you will say to someone
"someday"?
Why?
Make TODAY your most special day.
SOON is NOW!
SOMEDAY is NOW!
TOMORROW is HERE!
CELEBRATE TODAY!
DO IT TODAY! Yay!

Don't waste time

reliving your past or worrying
about what may happen
tomorrow. Simply relax into
the beauty of this Divine NOW
moment of your life and know
that only THIS moment is real.

In order to

fully express our true, authentic, Divine nature, we have to stop giving our power away to other people's fears, agendas, criticisms and opinions. It's time to OWN who we are and live free and clear of the outside noise and the need to conform. Take a STAND for who YOU uniquely are and live your life from YOUR heart and inner guidance as a full Divine expression of YOU. Beautiful, Divine YOU!

Oh just fricken
LEAP already!

Yup, that's how the messages are
coming through these days. No
excuses. No past stories and
patterns and self-imposed
limitations and self-doubt. YO!!!
It's TIME. Shed it. Let it go. Turn
on Your Heart Lights, Beautiful
Peeps. Shine it BRIGHT! The
WAVE is headed for shore.
SURF'S UP.
We are NOT in pre-game warm
up anymore.
And I gotta say it again…
IT'S SHOWTIME!! Woo Hoo!!

Trust

in the perfect Divine Standard
Timing (DST) & orchestration of
the Universe. You cannot miss out
on an opportunity, or a job, or an
important phone call that is yours
by Divine right. Trust that there is
a rhyme and a reason and that
something even BETTER is coming
to you. Relax. Take it easy. And get
into the DST time zone!

With each life

experience, we have the choice to
grab the golden nuggets or drag
around the boulders. We can tell
the same story over and over and
hold ourselves there or we can
say, "This is what I got from it,
this is what I gained and this is
who I am now because of it."
Be a Nuggeteer and grab your
Golden Life Experiences!

Embrace your fine,

Divine,

sublime self already

and BE IT!

Sometimes when

our dream is right in front of us, fears, unworthiness, insecurities, and doubts can come up. We can start mind-jerking our way out of it and looking for things that are wrong with us and/or others involved. Our upper limits of what we can have and deserve might be being tested… Can I really have it all? Do I really deserve this? Am I worthy of living my dream? If you have not worked on your beliefs and limitations and raise the ceiling limit you have placed upon yourself, you will surely find a way to sabotage it.

Isn't it time to EMBRACE THE DREAM and LIVE IT? Isn't it time to PLAY BIG and RELEASE all limitations and old baggage that binds you? There has never been a time when your dreams (the ones that are for the highest good of all concerned) can come to you faster and in more magical ways… that is if you ALLOW it. Soooooo whaaadddaya waiting for?

Isn't perspective

an interesting thing? Two people
can experience the exact same
event and see and feel two very
different things. And both will say
they are right. And from their
unique perspective and
experiences... they ARE.

If you are waiting

for the outer world to allow you
inner peace, you will be waiting a
long time. You will not find inner
peace by focusing on outer chaos.
Your ability to have inner peace is
entirely up to you and available
right NOW with a simple shift of
thought and focus. Aaaaah.
Now that's better!

What could you do

differently today that will make
"life as usual" even better?
Perhaps there is a pattern, belief
or behavior that you can shift.
Perhaps you will take a new turn
on a well-worn route. Perhaps
you will take a few moments
more to hug a tree or smell the
flowers. Whatever you do, do it
with love, intention,
presence and passion!

News Flash!

Moses was not the last person to
speak to God! Many miss the signs
and messages and whispers because
they are looking for a burning bush,
the sound of harps and singing
angels. Spirit speaks to us and
through us all day long in many
ways. Are you listening?

Questions to ponder:

Is this really true or am I making up
a story around it?

What is the truth without my beliefs
and perspectives and emotions
added on?

Is this for my highest good?

Is this the highest broadest story?

Is this an old story?

Does this serve me?

Is this on my Divine path?

Seek less...

BE more...

Anything anyone

has ever said and done to us either came from a place of love for us (even if we didn't understand their perspective or way of "loving") or from a place of disempowerment and not being able to love themselves. That means we get to let everyone off the hook who has ever said anything to us that we allowed to make us feel less than or limited. That means we get to let ourselves off the hook too because how it made us feel was just a story we made up at the time from our then perspective. We can change that story and all the beliefs we created around it from our NOW perspective... the now perspective that KNOWS the Divine, Worthy, Spiritual Being that we truly are.
We can now return to Love
for them and for ourselves.
Today is the day to Return to Love!

Everyone has

their own personal bubble through which we see physical reality. No matter what we say or do, others always filter it through their own perspective and belief system bubble. There are those that will find what is right with us and those that will find what is wrong with us ... and that is their reality based upon how they see the world, not yours. This is why it is so important to stay true to your core, to your heart, to YOU. If you let what others think enter your reality bubble, be sure that it resonates in your heart, otherwise you are allowing someone else's reality to become your own. Stay centered in Love even if others want to pop your bubble... because then your bubble becomes so filled with light that it raises above anything that is not Love. Up Up and Away!

When someone feels

the need to talk bad about you or try
turn others against you, they are only
showing their own insecurities,
jealousy and fears. Pay no mind.
Don't waste your precious time on
small thinking and judgmental,
disconnected people. There is no
need to defend yourself or engage in
smallness. Stand on the higher
ground and let VIBRATION do the
talking for you. Stand in your Light
with no need to fight… and leave the
drama behind. WAY behind.
Stay in LOVE and it just all works out
for the highest good!

If people are mean

or rude to you, instead of letting it trigger your own anger and lowering your vibration to match theirs, feel the compassion in your heart for this person that is obviously having an off day… or an off year, or whatever. Know that they would prefer to be happy but maybe just don't know how to get there. Perhaps your kindness, smile and high vibration is just what they need to make a shift.

From your unique

perspective and experiences you are always right, so it's okay to give up having to be right in the eyes of others, for they have their own unique perspectives and experiences. In having to be right and make others wrong, you give up your own emotional freedom and even physical health if you hold on to others wrongness and your rightness.
Relax and let them be right and stand true to your light.
You don't have to prove anything to the Universe or YOU!

It's not all

happening to us,

it's happening through us.

Download the Divine.

If you knew

the TRUE POWER your LOVE
emits in Frequency Waves and
God Particles to every other
being, plant, animal, tree, rock
and all in existence, you would
put up your antenna and start
broadcasting LOVE 24/7.

In every moment,

you have a choice about how
you feel. If you step back and
look through the wider
perspective of God/Spirit, you
will see the JOY in every
situation.
FEEL JOY NOW!

Seriously,

just don't take it all so
seriously! Be light, joyful,
forgiving, loving, giving
and you will find
lots to laugh about!

Some people say

It's "too hard" or they don't
have the time to deliberately
focus their thoughts and use a
daily spiritual practice to create
the life they want to live. But
isn't it even harder, more of a
struggle and time consuming to
live a life you don't want to live?
Just sayin'...

When you

completely stand in the LIGHT,
when LOVE is what Moves You and
Motivates You and Rules You, when
your True Intentions are for the
Highest Good of ALL Concerned
and you KNOW because you
KNOW because you KNOW that
EVERYTHING is ALWAYS in ALL
WAYS in Divine Order and Divinely
Orchestrated… you can relax into
any outcome without any need for
things to turn out in a certain way
and truly allow the Magic of the
Divine Universe to Flow through
YOU without resistance.
And that's when it gets REALLY
REALLY GOOD!

You have instant,

steady, always ready access to
Divine infinite intelligence at all
times through your inner
guidance and intuition.
Are you listening?

Before you act,

before you talk,

before you write, ask yourself,

"Does this come from a place of

inspiration and love? Does this

serve me and others?"

THEN act, talk and write!

All those

who belong in my Divine Life Story stay
All the others quickly and easily fade away

We all go on to our highest good
And as always things work out
just as they should

It's okay to let go and still love from afar
Releasing creates the space
to be who we really are

Out with the old, and in with the new
A new world of Divine experiences
are awaiting you

Trust Divine orchestration,
welcome the change
Act when inspired
and watch your life rearrange

Don't settle for less,
only the best and the highest will do
Embrace people and situations
that empower and inspire you

It's okay to leap, it doesn't matter how far
Have trust and faith
and be ALL that you ARE!

When we set

a clear intention for growth in one or more areas in our lives, what is not in alignment with our intention is often what presents itself to get transmuted and transformed. People often stop right there, mistakenly believing that roadblocks have been inserted. But really what is happening is that we are being shown the fastest, clearest road to get where we want to go; what needs to be cleaned up, where we are not a match to our desired outcome. Instead of taking a detour which will only lead to a circular road that is difficult to exit, observe what is being shown to clean up and lovingly clean it up! It's not a conspiracy against you; it's a conspiracy for you! It's not a roadblock, it's a shortcut! It's not a problem, it's an opportunity! Ahhh, yes, now we are on the High Road, straight ahead without speed limits.

Ah, yes,

the magic of Allowing… I don't think I even like the word manifesting anymore. That sounds like work. The real magic and easy FLOW is in ALLOWing your dreams into your life. FEELing worthy of them. KNOWing that the highest good will always happen. TRUSTing the Divine Timing and Orchestration. LISTENing to the messages, signs, impulses, intuitions. ACTing when Divine Inspiration hits. ENJOYing the Journey while nothing seems to be happening. (Oh, it is!) FOLLOWing YOUR Path. RELAXing into your dreams and visions without hesitation or resistance, cause it's already yours (as long as it is for the highest good of all concerned… but you know to ask for that from the beginning, right?)

You don't have to manifest anything. The Magical Universe does the manifesting work! You just ALLOW ALLOW ALLOW. NOW NOW NOW!

Many people want

to have their way with you…

It is about finding the people

whose "way" is Love…

Embrace the Divine

Spiritual Being that you are.
Embrace the stream of wellbeing
always flowing to you. Embrace
the magical, mysterious way the
Universe delivers your desires
when you focus on them without
resistance. Embrace Joy.
Embrace Love.
Embrace All that Is.
Embrace!

You don't

have to figure out HOW your
dreams will unfold... THAT is the
work of the powerful and magical
Universe... just get clear & keep
passionate about your dreams,
KNOW that you are worthy of
them, feel and act as you will feel
and act when they are already
yours and ALLOW the Universe to
do the how in ways you can't even
imagine! And remember to answer
the phone when it rings, follow up
on the leads and people who come
out of the blue and act on the
inspired ideas that will flow.

Let your Heart

be your GPS
(Guidance Positioning System).
Allow your Heart to guide you
to go left, go right,
make a legal U-turn or to
recalculate your route.
Put your Heart in the driver's
seat and you will always arrive
at your destination safely
and in Divine timing.

The beautiful thing

is that you don't have to figure
out HOW your dreams will
unfold... THAT is the work of the
Universe... just keep
PASSIONATE about your
dreams, KNOW that you are
worthy of them, FEEL as you will
feel when they are already yours,
take ACTION when inspired and
ALLOW the Universe to do the
HOW in ways you can't even
imagine!

Taking

"Leaps of Faith" is trust,

faith and Inspired Action

rolled into one.

It doesn't matter

if you believe in the LOA, the YMCA, the CIA, Cause and Effect, Evolution or Revolution… what matters is what works for you, what inspires you, what allows you to be at the Joy Set Point, the Zero Point of balance where your human self and spirit self are perfectly blended and expressed. (Yes, it's set at Joy!) The rabbit holes of the how's and why's and what happened's are never-ending deep, and while fun and fascinating to explore, hanging out in the JOY and LOVE of RIGHT NOW brings the most clarity of what it all means and why we are here.

If there is

someone that you cannot
forgive, it is wise to look at
where you are not forgiving
yourself. Where are you not
loving yourself enough to give
up holding on to negative
energy at your own expense in
all areas of your life?
Let it go. Lighten Up.
Fly FREE. The Shift is here.
Be Here NOW!
In LOVE.

Let go of anger,

resentment, blame and jealousy.
As long as we are holding onto
these emotions towards others,
we have not embraced the higher,
bigger picture and have not yet
taken the Divine gifts from the
relationship that are available to
us. Take a step back and let go of
the expectations of people having
to act a certain way for you to be
happy or feel good about
yourself. Being happy and feeling
good is an inner job. Let go of the
story, let go of the counter-
productive emotions that no
longer serve you and step into the
Universal Flow of Love.

Don't worry

about how it all works…

just WORK IT, Baby!

Often times

it is better to not say anything

at all until you can shift into

the place where I Love You

is all there is to say.

When stuff happens

I have five minutes of

"oh shit!"

and then comes the

"Oh! SHIFT!"

Playing

the Human Game with Joy while
remembering who you really are is
where you reach the BLISS STATE.
It's the best of the physical and the
non-physical, perfectly blended.
That's where you'll find me.

There really is

no heartbreak… only hearts
breaking open. Allow the so-called,
'heartbreaking' human experiences
break your heart WIDE OPEN and
to EXPAND… and let it then guide
you to Divine Inspired Action and
Unconditional Love.

When we are

in a place of pure unconditional
love, there is nothing to forgive
for we know everyone plays the
perfect part in our journey of
growth and expansion. Let
everyone off the hook and
beyond forgiveness, appreciate
them for playing their mutually
agreed upon role so perfectly. If
you are still holding on to what
others did to you, you have not
gathered up your golden nuggets
from the experience. Grab your
nuggets and return to LOVE!

It's always

good to check if the things that
you don't like in others aren't
things that bother you about
yourself... After all, those around
us are mirrors for us to look
through and sometimes it takes
others to hold up that mirror for
us to do some self-examination for
where we need more love for
ourselves and others.

Conflict.

Somehow many believe that we are supposed to live without conflict, but I look to nature and see what the animals do. Oh, yes, there is conflict in nature. I see the monkeys furiously fighting over food and territory and other issues — same with the macaws, dolphins, down to the hermit crabs. But the difference is in how they do it. They express themselves fully, they let it out, they GET ANGRY, and then they let it go. Five minutes later, they are swinging, swimming and pruning each other. Animals do not hold onto the anger because they have expressed it fully, said their truth and let it go. And THAT, baby, is how they do it on the Discovery Channel!

Before You Act

Before You Speak
Let the Universe Know
It's the Highest Good for All You Seek

Let Spirit Run Through You
Co-Create with the Divine
If You Relax and Let Go
It is Perfect Every Time!

You Don't Have to Push
You Don't Have to Shove
When You are Creating with Spirit
It's ALL about LOVE!

Have Compassion, Be Kind
For We Are All One
Allowing Other Aspects of Ourselves
Is All Part of the Fun

Let Go of Your Fears
The Past is the Past
Tell a New Story
One You Want to Last

And Most of All
Be True to YOU
That is the Best Way
To Let Spirit Shine Through!

We cannot be

responsible for other peoples'
happiness, nor they for ours. Any
time we depend on outside
circumstances or that people have
to act a certain way for us to be
happy, we are giving over our
power. Turn on your own inner
happiness and don't allow others
to depend on you for theirs.

It's a conspiracy!

Elite backroom deals…
people and things appearing
"out of the blue"…
strange sychronicities …
Yep, the whole Universe is
conspiring FOR you.

We are all

cosmically connected,

intrinsically intertwined,

eternally entangled...

and totally twisted...

You are not

the Creator, you are the Allower.
Everything you desire has already
been created and all you have to
do is believe, trust and allow it in!
THAT is co-creation in my book
(and I think we have the easy part!)

Our hearts never

forget but even the Masters
sometimes need to be
re-MINDed of our Divinity.
Surround yourself with people,
places and things that provide
constant re-MINDers of
Who You Really Are!

You can love

someone unconditionally and they still might not be a vibrational match to your inner circle people you keep close to you. Unconditional Love means you love the other person no matter what they are doing and also love YOU enough to remove yourself when the relationship or situation doesn't feel right. You can love someone unconditionally and still not want to be in the vicinity of their behaviors. Learn to say, "I love you and see you around!"

I now release

all thoughts that no longer

serve me. I let them go.

Easily and effortlessly.

And I replace them with

thoughts of what I truly desire.

In fact, I BECOME that now!

Expect Lucky,

Expect Charmed, Expect Easy,
Expect Success, Expect Blessed,
Expect the Best, Expect Fun... and
then get out of the way, forget
about the how's and the when's
and let the Universe top your
expectations every time!

Forget

Pacific Standard Time (PST).
I run on DST (Divine Dolphin
Standard Time). DST means
that everything happens
exactly when it should and I
just get to relax and let it
unfold in Divine orchestration
and timing. Everyone switch
to DST and life becomes
relaxed and easy!
Woo Hoo!

What do you

REALLY want?

Get clear,

and the Universe

will clear the way!

Our work is to

observe our non-serving
behaviors and patterns without
getting pulled in and triggered.
We observe and catch ourselves
in the act of running old
patterns and behaviors and
LOVINGLY shift them into
new behaviors and patterns
that serve our highest good.
Name em', claim em', shift em'!
Be a conduit of Love and the
highest good for yourself and
for others.

People often say,

"When I win the lottery…"
literally putting all the ways and
means to their dreams in one
basket. Don't limit the Infinite
Universe with only one route to
provide to you. It's all the
Universal Lottery Jackpot when
you consciously create what you
want with your imagination,
feelings and inspired actions, no
matter how it gets to you.
Dream and Live your Dream
Now. And let the Universe
deliver the Mega Powerball!

We ALL need

to be re-MINDED,

but never re-HEARTed...

If we look

at observing and shifting our
limiting beliefs as an exciting
journey towards expansion and
enlightenment and not a dark,
scary, difficult past to face, think
of what we can easily let go of...
and who we can now be!
Let facing and identifying
limiting beliefs & hidden
emotions be an exciting
expansion into who you really
are. Nothing to be afraid of and
everything to become and gain!

Do you know

how powerful, unique,

amazing and Divine you are?

You are ALL that and so much

more… Embrace it, baby!

The relationships

you attract into your life
are a direct reflection of the
amount of love and worthiness
you feel for yourself.

Sure there are

things I would have done

differently knowing

what I know now…

Bbut I wouldn't know what I

know now if I had done

things differently…

When YOU

and the YOUniverse are in
congruence; that is, your Body,
Mind and Spirit are aligned
and in agreement, not even
wild horses can drag magical
circumstances and outcomes
even better than you can
imagine, away from you.

Let there be

relationships where there is
no drama, jealousy, judgment
and game playing. Let there
be relationships where we
only want and wish the best
and highest good for all
concerned as we know that
their highest good and
success is our highest good
and success. Let there be
authentic, real, honest
communication
from the heart.
And let it begin with me.

We are creators

in our reality because we have the choice of where to put our thoughts and focus about anything that is going on in our lives and in the world. Everything is a neutral experience until we put our beliefs and perspective upon it. That is our creative power, the vibration that results from what we give our focus, passion and attention to. What are you creating today?

You get

what you settle for. You get
what you focus on and think
about, whether you want it
or not. You get what you
believe you deserve. Who
and what shows up in your
life exactly mirrors your B.S.
(Belief Systems).
Shift your B.S.
and shift your world!

Allow the Universe

to give you what is already yours
by Divine birthright. You are
worthy, you are deserving, you
are Love, you ROCK!
Why not live the life you want to
live? Let go of the doubts and
worries and fears and step right
into Living Life Out Loud!

There are infinite

amazing opportunities and
experiences to say YES! to in this
World. Say YES to JOY! Say YES
to BLISS! Say YES to NATURE!
Say YES to Authentic Human
Experiences! Say YES to
LETTING GO! Say YES to Divine
Orchestration and Timing! Say
YES to OWNING your
DIVINITY!
Say YESSSSSSSSSSSSSSSSS
to LOVE!!
What are YOU
saying YES! to today?

Give the gift

of your true

authentic self

to the world!

The story

you tell to yourself and to
others is where you hold
yourself. Is the story you are
telling over and over the one
you want to be creating? If not,
tell a new story and watch
how quickly things change!

The things

that manifest best and fastest are
the things you are naturally
passionate about, without having
to try. The things that make your
heart sing and your toes wiggle
are things that Spirit is leading
you to, so everything goes
perfectly when you follow
THOSE. Passionate inspired
desires are the ones that manifest
like magic because you don't
have to try to get into the feeling
place. You are already there!

Whether you look

for what's wrong, or what's right...

you'll always find it...

Love is

the Universal Language that is
inter-species, inter-religion,
inter-race, inter-political party,
and inter-beliefs. If we all
speak the language of Love,
the lines of communication are
always open between
everyone and everything.

You have done

nothing wrong. There have been
no mistakes. Everything that has
happened has perfectly led up to
this now moment when you can
choose to embrace your divinity.
It's all okay, there is nothing you
need to make up for or fix. You
can proudly shine your light right
now. You can choose right now to
accept all of what it means to be a
human and from here you can fly.
From here you can live a life
extraordinary. Right NOW!

By looking

at something you don't want and saying over and over "I don't want this" (and blogging about it, complaining to all your friends about it and joining organizations AGAINST it), you are bringing more of what you don't want into your experience. Instead, take a quick look at what you don't want and then focus and talk about and dream about the things that what you don't want have caused you to WANT.

We can get lost

in the story about what happened
and what they did and what they
didn't do, but the healing and shift
comes when you get to the core of
how what happened made you
FEEL — and take responsibility for
your feelings. Forget the story and
any power you have given others
over you with the blame or anger.
Get to the core of "I didn't feel
loved," "I didn't feel appreciated,"
or "I didn't feel safe," and make
your shift from the place of being
responsible for your own loving,
appreciation and safety.
YOU HAVE THE POWER!
Lose the story, get to the core, and
take your power back!

As I focus

on what I want and feel the
feelings of already being that
and having that, I am led
along a magical path of Divine
unfoldings that takes me on
the most direct, fast and fun
route to get there!

The only karma

that exists is that which we
impose upon ourselves by
carrying around guilt and
shame from the past. Clear
your Karma now and let
yourself off the hook!

If we are

still holding someone's toes to
the fire for something they did
in the past, we are not allowing
them the same space we want
for ourselves to grow and
expand. We've all done things
we would do differently now
from our new place of BEing,
learning and expanding…
So, let it go and allow others
to re-create themselves and
become NEW Beings too! See it
all through the eyes of Love
and no one gets burned.

You never

have to be what other people
expect you to be or live up to
other's expectations of who you are
or who you're not. That's their
story, not yours. You never have to
judge yourself or change yourself
based on someone else's
perception and beliefs. Their
perceptions and beliefs are based
on their experiences, not yours. Be
100% true to you. Don't hold back
because of fear of judgment or
what others will say or think. That
is living your life for others. It's
time to step up. It's time to shift.
It's time to claim your true
authentic self and BE it with pride
and joy. Shine the light YOU came
to shine. It's SHOWTIME, baby!

Are you running

Windows98 in a 2013 world? Just like a computer, humans run on the "software" they were programmed with in their early years of development. Some humans choose to upgrade as they have new and different experiences and take the best and leave the rest... and some people keep running the same old patterns and programs even though new information is available. And I am here to say… BABY, IT'S TIME TO UPGRADE!!! Let go of the old, no longer relevant to NOW programming and upgrade your human software! Do a disk scan, delete all impertinent and irrelevant data based on old programming and thinking, Reboot and INSTALL the latest… HUMAN2.0! It may take a little getting used to like any new computer program does, but once you know your way around all the bells and whistles, you are going to LOVE the NEW UPGRADED YOU!!

When people call

you selfish, isn't it that they want

you to act in a way that is

pleasing to THEM and makes

THEM happy? So who is the

selfish one? Just sayin'.

When it comes

to opinions and perspectives, from your unique life experiences you are always right, so it's okay to give up having to be right in the eyes of others, for they have their own unique perspectives and life experiences. In having to be right and make others wrong, you give up your own emotional freedom and even physical health if you hold on to others wrongness and your rightness. Relax and let them be right and stand true to YOUR light. You don't have to prove anything to anyone except to stay true to you. When you stand in your Light without a fight you are always RIGHT!

Spiritual knowledge

is great and all, but it's when you
BECOME and INTEGRATE the
knowledge into your daily life that
true magic happens...

If you stop

repeating all the stories you tell
about your health, relationships
and financial situation stop
recounting the past and what so
and so did, stop worrying about
the future and judging everyone,
all that is left is to talk from your
heart/love space about the
present moment and unfolding
dreams. Or perhaps entertain not
talking at all and silently basking
in the energy and beauty around
you… and listening to the
whispers and messages of Spirit.

Expectations.

We all got em'. People expect things of us, we expect things of others. And when the reality doesn't match our expectations we can either choose to be disappointed and angry, or we can open up our minds and hearts and know that everyone and everything is Divinely perfect just as it is.

Whenever I talk

to the animals about ascension, they laugh and say, "Why do humans always think that somewhere else is better? Do you think The Great Spirit put us here on this amazing planet so that we can ascend away from here? We think not. Your paradise is here. Your paradise is within. You can embrace it anytime. The only thing you have to ascend is your own fears and to remember who you truly are. THAT is ascension. The animals are not trying to ascend. We are balancing energies, caring for this planet and living in the right NOW."

Let it go.

Let go of the blame, let go
of the guilt, let go of the
need to know, let go of the
hurt, sorrow, hate, anger
and self-doubt. Let it all go
and set yourself free!

I easily let go

of old beliefs and habits and
patterns. It's not who I am
now. Every day, I release
more of my beliefs that limit
me. I become more and
more unlimited now!

If your own cup

is running over, you then
have so much more to give
to others. Fill your cup first,
take care of yourself, do
things that bring you joy,
and others will benefit from
your self love and
appreciation overflow.

As soon

as you try to define something,
you have put it in a box. The less
you try to define it, the more open
and unlimited are the
possibilities. Un-define your
mind and watch new possibilities
appear that your previous
definitions didn't allow.
Open, Open, OPEN

Spirituality

has become a religion in some ways as everyone compares their way of "connecting" and what is the right best way to get "there." But everyone in every moment has the capacity to get "there" with no tools or tricks. Yesa, they are fun, they create uniqueness and variety and it's ALL Divine. But let go of the "rules" and "separation" and '"competition' around them. Everyone goes where tthey are divinely guided. Ceremony and ritual and methods are all good if done with joy and creative Divine expression. But it is never necessary or required to get to a certain place. If anyone tells you that you need a certain ritual or tool or teacher, they have missed the point.

We can choose

to love, we can choose to hate, we can choose to celebrate. It's all part of the experience we chose to participate in from our non-physical perspective. And when we finally choose to equally blend our Body~Mind~Spirit and embrace our true Triune self, we remember that it's all for the fun of it, all for the expansion of it, all for the LOVE of it.

You can never

go wrong asking for the

highest good for all concerned.

Whether through

meditation, dance, song, prayer
or skipping stones, make a
conscious daily practice of
connecting to Spirit. . .

The Universe

is always working for you,
not against you. Go ahead
and surrender to its
outrageous magnificence.
Allow the Universe to
take care of everything.
It just feels soooo good
to let go and trust!

You know

what they say...
Wait!!
Who is "*they*" and why listen
to "*them*" when YOU are the
creator of your life? If you
listen to what "*they*" say, you
will get the life that
"*they*" want you to lead.

Be it NOW!

What would your actions,
thoughts, and words be right
NOW if you were the person
you want to be
(and really already are?)

We are never

given dreams or desires that
we cannot achieve. Forget
about the how and when and
focus on your dreams and
desires. There are no limits on
what is possible as long as you
get out of the way and let the
Universe deliver to you!

When we are

in a place of Unconditional Love, we only see LOVE or those wanting/needing Love. No Good, Bad, or Wrong. Just Love or the Illusion of Lack of Love. That's all there is.

Whenever you find

yourself saying, "I think…"
change it instead to, "I feel…"
and get into your Heart Space
and out of your Head Space.
Instead of asking, "What do you
think?" ask, "What do you
FEEL?" In other words, STOP
THINKING and START
FEELING!
Ride the Wave! FEEL the wave!!

Do you focus

on or worry about the worse
case scenario or do you
think about and focus on the
best possible outcome for all
concerned?
Hint: it makes a big
difference in the outcome!

You can find

happiness right now by letting
go of the "shoulds" and
"shouldn'ts" you've put on
YOU! You are Divine, Sacred,
and truly God's hands in action
through the physical. You can
choose to stop suffering right
now by not entertaining your
inner judge. Release all
"shoulds" around your life
today and notice how free and
easy you feel! By the way,
there's only one "should"...
Everything is exactly as it
"should" be!

As a non-physical

being you said: I shall go forth
into the physical and expand the
leading edge of thought and ALL
THAT IS thru my human
experiences. I shall choose the
parents, friends, lovers and
experiences that allow me to love,
laugh, cry, feel bliss, feel angry; all
which will cause me to expand
and grow. I shall take none of it
too seriously because I willingly
and excitedly signed up for this as
a Special Agent of Spirit...
Remember?

You are always

Divinely Guided. An ever-present
Loving Universal Super
Intelligence is always guiding you
to manifest your dreams, desires,
happiness, and life purpose. Divine
Spirit is always calling you forward
towards Love and Divine
Expression. Trust this Truth and
know that when you truly listen to
your Heart you are always
Divinely Guided. Pay attention, be
present, observe and allow your
Divine Guidance to show you the
easiest and quickest path to your
true purpose and highest good.

Life is like a radio

station, and you are the DJ.

What you broadcast is the

feedback you get.

So put another record on, baby!

Never, ever EVER

doubt the POWER of your passion,
focus, Love, intentions, Light. YOU,
YOU, YOU are as important and
divine as the smallest amoeba to the
grandest blue whales to the richest of
the rich to the masters of the Masters.
YOU, YOU, YOU are as much as part
of the Divine Web of All That Is as
anything and anyone.

So start acting like it. BE IT
ALREADY. We are in the time of
intense change and transformation.
What are YOU contributing to the
WHOLE? To the Highest GOOD for
ALL Concerned?

Practice time is over.
IT'S SHOWTIME, BABY.

About the Author

Sierra Goodman is a woman who truly follows and lives her dreams. From her ocean front rainforest property on Costa Rica's Osa Peninsula — known as the most biologically-intense place on Earth, both on land and at sea — Sierra inspires thousands of people daily with her unique insight, clarity, wisdom and humor through her Facebook page, blog and contributions to books, articles, websites and interviews. Sierra teaches us about living the authentic human experience with ease and joy, natural weight loss (she lost 170 pounds in one year (see: www.iam-iam-iam.com), as well as sharing insights on her beloved finned family, the dolphins and whales.

She also has the JOB (Joy of Being) of facilitating life-changing trips by taking humans to swim with and experience the unbounded Joy and Love of the wild dolphins and whales in Bimini Bahamas,

Silver Bank Dominican Republic and at her home in Drake Bay, Costa Rica. See her website at www.divinedolphin.com.

Now Sierra's evolving wisdom has perpetuated the creation of the *Oceans of Inspiration* series of products featuring her Heart-Inspired quotes coupled with her breathtaking and world-famous photos and videos of dolphins, whales and other nature beings. You can enjoy screensavers, coffee mugs, t-shirts, digital photo frames and an upcoming coffee table book with your favorite *Oceans of Inspiration* quotes.

Sierra has learned to hear and follow her inner guidance and intuition and take inspired action on the messages, or *Echoes of the Heart*, that she receives. She attributes her knowledge of the Universal Laws and a lot of quiet time in nature to her ability to connect deeply with 'All That Is' and express what she hears in words that inspire others. And that it inspires others greatly inspires her. It's always a win-win when we follow our highest good and express our true, authentic self freely and with love and joy.

For more on *Oceans of Inspiration*, visit: www.oceansofinspiration.com.

Made in the USA
Middletown, DE
23 December 2018